THE TIMES OF INDIA

SIGNS OF THE TIMES

Signs of the Times

First Edition 2010

Published by
Ravi Dhariwal for the proprietors,
Bennett, Coleman & Co. Ltd.,
New Delhi

Edited, Designed, Marketed & Distributed by

Times Group Books

Times Group Books
(A division of Bennett, Coleman and Company Limited)
Times Annexe, 9-10, Bahadur Shah Zafar Marg, New Delhi-110002

Printed at: Raveindia

ISBN 978-81-89906-90-0
Price: Rs.295
Send your feedback at: editor.tgb@timesgroup.com

Preface

On September 7, 2008, The Sunday Times of India carried a strategically placed, small yellow box on its news pages. It read as follows: "What's the funniest, silliest, most extraordinary sign you've seen on India's roads? Amusing names of villages or talukas; absurd English translations, graphical gaffes. Get signspotting and send us your entries — a photograph and brief description telling us where and what it is. Each week, the three best entries will win an attractive prize from Magpie, the kitchenware company. We'll carry the pick of the lot in the next edition of the Sunday Times."

The invitation was positioned below a photograph advertising "Child Bears" on NH-8. The misspelt advert for chilled beer said it all about signage in our great and glorious country. From then on, there was no stopping our readers. Every week, we had hundreds of entries, choosing the wittiest, weirdest, whackiest or most wonderful to publish. We moved rapidly through a sign for the railway station with the longest name (Venkatanarasimharajuvaripeta on the Chennai-Tirupati route) through to a little-known example of hospitality with one eye on Sino-Indian ties (the last Indian dhaba on the border with China in Chitkul, which has a population of just 610). Some signs were just plain funny, as in the offer of "ladies bottoms" for Rs 199 in Kolkata.

Two years and hundreds and hundreds of readers' entries later, we can reveal that each photograph prompted us to ask ourselves the most obvious question in this age of technological progress and prowess: Is it photoshopped? We tried to strip out the obvious imposters and think we found genuine gems that capture the essence of India's sign language and conversation with itself. In the process, Signs of the Times became something of an institution. Here by popular demand, a keepsake selection of some of the best.

Rashmee Roshan Lall
Editor, Sunday Times of India

CHEAP AT ANY PRICE

Seen on a footpath in Chowringhee, Kolkata, by Anuradha Roy.

RARE HALF-PRICE DEAL

Seen in a shop in Nerul, Mumbai, by K. Raghu Raman.

INDIA VOTES FOR THE IRRESISTIBLE REPUBLICAN DISH

Seen outside a canteen at the Mysore Zoo, by Malini Rajesh.

THE EASY WAY TO THE BIG APPLE

This photograph of a real milestone was taken on NH-8 on the way from Udaipur to Ajmer, by Manoj Kumar & S.N. Ahmad.

SNAKES FOR SNACKS? CLEAR YOUR DOUBTS BEFORE ORDERING!

Seen on a street side shop in T.Nagar, Chennai, by S.Muthukaruppan.

SINGH IS RISKY AFTER WHISKY:
A CAUTION ISSUED FOR PUBLIC SAFETY

Seen on the highway while driving from Agra to Kanpur, by Sudeep Singh.

BANANA REPUBLIC

A handicapped vendor's observation 'HANDI-CAPPED GOVT. OF INDIA' — is it a mistake or the vendor just wanted to point out the truth. Seen at Chembur, Mumbai, by Arun A. Bahl.

TUITIONS ON PLANET TEN—WONDER WHAT THE FEE WILL BE!

Seen outside an institute that attracts "studets" in Vijay Nager, New Delhi, by Devesh Pratap Singh.

RUNOVER RULES: HOPE BMW DRIVERS PAY HEED!
Seen in Bangalore, by Ramesh Kumar.

TRAFFIC SIGNS
Know them. Follow them.
They're good omen
Spotted by Jensil John.

PUNCTURED SPELLINGS

A vulcanising shop seen at Varadhapalayam, enroute to Sri Kalahasthi, by P.L. Ramanathan.

MISSPELT BUS SHELTERS: WORKING FOR PEOPLE THOUGH

The Greater Noida Authority gets it all wrong. Snap 1. shows "Collectrade" instead of Collectorate. Snap 2. shows "Fare Station" in place of Fire Station. Seen on the Surajpur-Kasna Road, Greater Noida, by Surendra Chaudhary.

WELCOME TO THE WASHROOM: A RELIEF ON THE HIGHWAY

Spotted on G.T. Karnal road on way to Jalandhar from Delhi, by Nikhil Athwani.

PLUMBING PROBLEMS? NO PROBLEM.
HERE'S THE MAN WITH SOLUTIONS.

A hillarious description of a plumber's shop. Spotted in Juhugali, Andheri (West), Mumbai, by Vikas G. Nayak.

NO NO THEY ARE NOT SELLING IT HERE

It's a way to a gents restroom
Spotted a gents urinal on NH-7 on the Mumbai-Bangalore highway,
by Ashwin Kuckian.

CIVIL ASSISTANT SURGEON — WONDER WHAT DOES THAT MEAN

Seen in the busy market of Hosur, Tamil Nadu,
by Ashwin Kuckian.

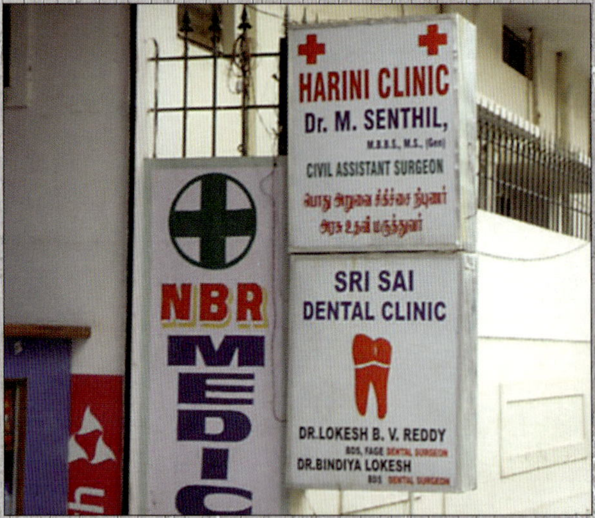

HERE ANGELS FEAR TO TREAD

A strong message to those who park in front of the gates of houses. Spotted on Mannagudda New Road in Mangalore, Karnataka, by Dr. Manohar Balge.

NO PARTIALITY WITH THE DRIVER PLEASE!

Seen in an autorickshaw in Delhi, by Davinder.

HOT DEALS ON HOT WHEELS

Never mind the spellings, rooms are available!
Spotted on a pick-up tempo in Bangalore, by Dr Sunil Furtado.

FILL UP, THEN RIDE — *CLEAR HAI!*
Seen at a petrol pump in south Delhi, by Gaurav Singh.

AMERICAN TASTE. DESI STYLE.

This sweet corn seller has everything to challenge the American economy. Seen in Tilak Nagar, Delhi, by Avneesh Chhabra.

CAUTION WITH CREATIVITY AT 18380FT ABOVE SEA LEVEL

With the highest motorable road in the world, Ladakh at 18380 ft above sea level is also known for its road signs. Clicked by Vinayak Kulkarni.

MUST BE A JOKE! SERIOUSLY

Spotted by Amit Merwar.

MEN WILL BE MEN

This roadside dhaba's urinal for gents was seen somewhere in Solapur, Maharashtra, by Kiron Thakore.

AN ERRONEOUS START TO A MARRIAGE

The photograph of this marriage hall was taken from a bus while travelling from Bangalore to Mysore, by Uttam Saxena.

DOES THIS STOP YOU IN YOUR TRACKS?

This Railway Station has the longest name in the country. Seen on the Chennai-Tirupati route, by Deepak Mallik.

HOUSEFULL AT THIS LUXURY RESORT

This photograph taken in May 2007 captures some unlikely tourists at the tourist home at Sendra Island in Loktak Lake, Manipur, by Prabanee Sarmah.

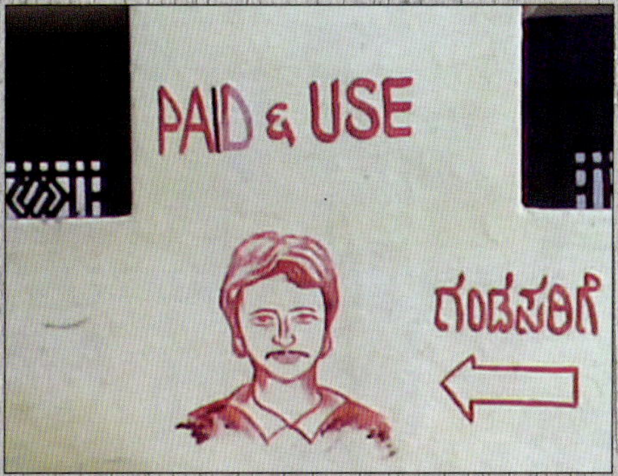

PAY N' PASS

This photograph is of the only and dirty toilet taken at Dhavengere Railway Station, by Vivek.

THIS PLACE SURELY GIVES KFC A RUN FOR THEIR MONEY

Seen in Delhi by Asmita Laskar.

'OOOOFS' WHAT A 'FITY' — HOPE THE PEDESTRIANS DON'T MIND!

Guess, something to do with the ascent! Seen at the Old Hubli bus stand, by Vivek.

HOPE THEIR FURNITURE IS BETTER THAN THEIR SPELLINGS

This signboard was spotted outside a furniture seller/hirer at Infantry Road, Bangalore by Arun Bhatia.

PARKING PROBLEMS ON EARTH

Looks like this one has a solution. Spotted by Raj Gandhi.

A CHANGE IN ATTITUDE

It actually changes the whole meaning of the original quote! This photograph was taken while travelling in a HRTC (Himachal Road Transport Corporation) Bus in the Lahaul & Spiti region of Himachal Pradesh, by Navneet

IS NOT HOOTCH, JUST EXTREMELY CHILLED BEER. ARE YOU GAME?

A hoarding used by a 'theka' (Wine and Beer Shop) to attract customers. Spotted on the G T Karnal Road in Haryana, by Ravneek Wadhwa.

MEL BROOKS, MEL GIBSON, MEL BROWN...
IS EVERYONE READY HERE?

This signboard was seen outside an eatery on the highway from Belgaum to Amboli, by Shailesh R. Sanzgiri.

RULES ARE RULES

This one clearly defines all clauses.
This signboard was spotted on a tree at a tea stall on the road from Manali to the Rohtang pass, by Arvind Swadi.

TOO HOT AN OFFER

Fully sold out! Seen at a shop at the Metro Walk Mall at Rithala, Delhi, by V.M. Govind Krishnan.

THE ROAD TO BEING A YANKEE...

This milestone was seen on the way to Shivanasamudra Waterfalls, a few kms from Bangalore, by Rudram Reddy.

THE FOOD DEPT. SHOULD HAVE PUT THEIR BEST FOOT FORWARD

This photograph was taken at the Chennai Trade Center, Chennai, by Ajay Aurora.

SHAVE AND SAVE

Spotted by Mithilesh Sawanth.

DON'T LET THE SPELLING BOTHER YOU IF THE BEER IS CHILLED

Seen in the small town of Naggar, near Manali, Himachal Pradesh, by Vikas G. Nayak.

DON'T TRY TO READ AND INTERPRET. JUST ASK!

They have Xerox for sure. For all other services kindly ask. Seen at NH-7, by Basant Singh.

WHICH SIDE ARE YOU ON?

This photograph was taken on NH-1, Jammu-Srinagar highway, by Neha Raina.

THE DEMON OF SPEED BITES BAD — AN INNOVATIVE WARNING.

Better drive slowly or be bitten by a cobra! This signboard was seen 5 kms ahead of Narendra Nagar in Uttarakhand, by Sanjeev & Nibha Vyas.

ONE INDIA MANY RELIGIONS

Whatever be the religion, an Indian is an Indian. This photograph was taken on the Leh-Srinagar highway, by Rohan Mozumdar.

WASHROOM VERSE RESTROOM RECKONER

An innovative signage for public toilet hygiene seen at a restaurant in Manipal, by Dr Rohit Singh.

HOPE THEY GET GENUINE CUSTOMERS

Anyone interested in Genuine fakes? This shop was spotted on the road leading to Calangute in Goa, by Gurdeep Singh.

LOVE YOUR SPOUSE NOT SPEED

This signboard was spotted on the road leading to Indo-Bhutan border, in western Bhutan , by Munjal Adhvaryu.

YOUR KIDS LEARN SAFETY FROM YOU.

Seen on the side of a small street in Mangalore, Karnataka, by Dr. Rohit Fernandez.

SAFETY FIRST: EVEN ON WORLD'S HIGHEST MOTORABLE ROAD.

A signboard put up by the Border Roads Organisation. Seen on the Khardugla-Nubra (Ladakh) Road, by Jaideep Khodaskar.

A DIFFERENT DATE

Have a delicious date with your family! Spotted on the highway between Ghaziabad and Hapur, by Nitin Goyal.

HOOK, LINE AND STINKER!

Seen at Sahid Nagar, Bhubaneswar, Orissa, by Akshyaya Kumar Behera.

FOOD FOR THOUGHT

Still feeling hungry? It's totally your call whether you want to get into a delicious mess. Seen in JP Nagar, Bangalore, by Vidya Baliga.

BRAND CONSCIOUS SHOPPER'S PARADISE

This unique shop was spotted in Calangute, Goa, by Daphne.

WEIGHTY INSTRUCTIONS

Spotted on Pandara Road, New Delhi, by Bhavna Dagar.

GET STRESSED AT YOUR OWN RISK

Seen on a street in a friendly neighbourhood, by Pradeep Kalala Sudarshan.

AN APPRECIATED GESTURE

Wonder if they are trying to impress the National Commission for Women!
This photograph was taken in August 1995 on a trip to Kodaikanal, by Aparna Datta.

NO OFFENCE MEANT TO YOUR EXTENDING WAISTLINE.

Seen in the forest of Kodaikanal, by Vijay Narayanan.

TIFFIN READY: THAT'S WHAT THEY MEANT

This picture of a hoarding was taken in Thiruparangkundram, Madurai by Rajgovind J.

CAPITAL MISTAKE: A NATIONAL SHAME

Seen at Apollo Flyover, New Delhi, by Anshuman Gupta.

ACTUALLY, IT IS THIS HELPLINE THAT NEEDS HELPPPPPPP!

A school van carrying children to school. Spotted in Saket, New Delhi, by Tushar Singhal.

SPELL LIKE YOU PRONOUNCE

Snacks served with a southy touch!

Seen at a roadside fastfood outlet in Munnar, Kerala, by Hareish Makhija.

WHIRLPOOL CAUTION: TAKE THE WARNING SERIOUSLY NOT THE SPELLING

This warning was found on a rock beside a pond near the famous Hanuman temple in Hampe, by BLR Ravi.

REQUESTING FOR SILENCE THE IRANIAN WAY

A picture of an instruction seen in an Irani restaurant in Mahim, Mumbai, by Swapnali Das.

STILL WAITING FOR THE STRIPES?

Spotted an advertisement outside a 'Sahakari Bhandar' outlet in Mumbai, by H.S. Bhatia.

JUST A REMINDER — WALKING'S NOT GOOD ALWAYS!

Seen on the way to Ranikhet, Uttarakhand, by Rajesh Gupta.

PEEING ISSUES: IS ANYBODY HEARING?

This warning was spotted near Universal Bakers in KPHB colony, Kukatpally, Hyderabad, by Tushar Patil.

SCHOOL SHOOT-OUT CASES NOT OUR CUP OF TEA

Spotted a notice put up at the gate of an elite school in Mohali, Punjab, by Abhay Vikram.

SANITATION ISSUES AT HEIGHTS.

Seen in a monastery in Leh, Ladakh, by Nameeta Prakash.

THEY DON'T PUNCH EARS HERE. JUST REPAIR FLAT TYRES.

This picture was taken on a road near Yeshwantpur, Bangalore, by Suvam Nandi.

HOPE THE METER READING IS NOT AS FAULTY AS ITS SPELLING

Seen on a meter box of an autorickshaw in Mulund [West], Mumbai, by Snehrag Raghavan.

ARRANGED LOVE: THE MATCHMAKER'S PROMISE

Seen on a wall opposite Karjat Station, 85km from Mumbai, by Glenn.

A WHEELING MISTAKE: DON'T WORRY THE RATES ARE FOR VEHICLES

This signage was spotted near Himayat Nagar, Hyderabad, by Michelle Signature.

HEALTHY TRUCK TALK: BEWARE OF DANGEROUS DISTRACTIONS

Seen on a highway near Nasik, by Sonia Augustine.

SURELY ! MR GATES MUST HAVE OVERLOOKED THIS ON HIS TRIP TO INDIA

Seen at Borgaon village, on way from Chhindwara to Nagpur, by Jatinderpal Sngh Uppal.

IS CHINA TAKING OVER THE INDIAN 'CUTTING-CHAI'?

Spotted in Mumbai by K. Aarthi Priyadarshini.

AN IDENTITY CRISIS

What's in a name! The owner of this eatery in Dharmshala, Himachal Pradesh, seems to be highly inspired by Shakespeare.

TAKE THE STAIRS...THE BEST WAY TO REACH CHINA

Hope the Chinese don't read this! Seen outside a restaurant in Panchgani ,Maharashtra, by Zubair Shariff.

IT'S JUST A SURNAME STUPID

Seen outside the District Commissioner's office in Tawang ,Arunachal Pradesh, by Brikesh.

THE SECRET TO A BILLION POPULATION

Seen on the streets of Jaisalmer, Rajasthan, by Sachin Mundra.

IT MUST BE TOUGH LIVING UP TO THIS SURNAME

Spotted by Kanishka.

NOW YOU KNOW WHY BENGAL BACKED DIDI

Bottom business busted! Pushing too far these elections. Seen in the bylanes of Kolkata by Chidanad Kumar.

QUITE INTERESTING THIS — HOT MALE SERVED! WHO NEEDS A HOT MEAL? RIGHT GIRLS!

Spotted by Arvind Bharti.

A RISKY INVITE TO A RIDE

Seen by Dr. Srirang Akbari.

FOLLOW INSTRUCTIONS AT YOUR OWN PERIL

Thoughtfully, the authorities have indicated how tough they were with people who follow their instructions. This instruction was seen at Mysore Zoo, by SV Sreeram.

AN UNPRODUCTIVE ADVERTISEMENT

A notice put up opposite Old Fort near Delhi Zoo, inviting applications for Government work. Spotted by George L. Samte.

TO BE OR NOT TO BE ALLOWED

Seen at Mysore, by Maanya Ravindra.

LISTEN UP! IT'S DIVINE ADVICE

Not everyone gets a second chance! Seen at Visakhapatnam, Andhra Pradesh, by Maneesh Upmanyu.

A HEAVEN FOR CAR THIEVES

Spotted at the parking area of Metro Station of Sector-10, Dwarka, New Delhi, by Narendra Soni.

MATHURA GATE: A HOLY MISTAKE

Seen at a Police Station in Bharatpur (Rajasthan), by Udoy Bhaskar Borah.

ALL ROADS LEAD HOME

This picture was taken at 'Maitri', the India Research Station at Antarctica, by Rajeev Nayak.

THE DOCTOR'S NAME SPEAKS OF HIS SPECIALIZATION

Seen in a town in Kerala, by Subash C.

TO ERR IS DIVINE

Seen outside the Afghan Church in Mumbai, by Renu Singh Majji.

NOW THAT'S A TRAFFIC STOPPER

Spotted on a highway by Zubair Shariff.

WHAT'S IN A NAME?

Seen in Bangalore, by Nithya Dakshinamoorthy.

AND HOW ABOUT TRESPASSERS?

Seen at a construction site near Hyderabad, by Vinod Kumar M.

STATUTORY WARNING: LIKE YOU'VE NEVER SEEN BEFORE

Spotted in Bangalore, by SN Murthy.

RANG DE: A LAUNDRY THAT NAILS ITS COLOURS TO THE MAST

Seen in Kolkata, by Kuo Shane.

SINGH IS KING EVEN WHEN IT COMES TO SELLING FASHION

Seen in Pondicherry, by K A Somaiah.

JUNK FOOD WITH A HEALTH WARNING

Seen in Tamil Nadu, by Saurabh Raghuwanshi.

A STITCH IN TIMES

Seen in Kammanahali, Bangalore, by Jerin Xavier.

GO WITH THE FLOW

Seen outside the Mantralayam Temple in Andhra Pradesh, by Vishwas MG.

NOW THAT'S A REAL DEAL

Seen in Nagpur, by Sandeep V Bhageshwar.

FAST AND COURTEOUS

Spotted on an autorickshaw in Hampi, Karnataka, by Arindam Chatterjee.

THE HANGOVER

A photograph of the signboard put up by the Bangalore Traffic Police as part of a road safety awarness drive in the city, by Yatin Jai Singh.

FREUDIAN SLIP IN AAMCHI MUMBAI

An MNS poster pasted by Raj Thackeray suppoters over an English coaching class advert, ends up conveying a confusing message. Seen near Virar Railway Station, Mumbai, by Ashish Vartak.

ABSTAIN TO ATTAIN NIRVANA

Seen in Chennai, by Bernadette Lobo.

WHILE DRIVING ON INDIAN ROADS

Seen on NH-4 between Haveri and Hubli, Karnataka, by Jagadeesh Magavi.

LOOKS LIKE A WARNING

Seen in Delhi by Amarpreet Singh.

WHO'S FOOLING WHOM?

Seen in a bazaar of Hyderabad, by K Sridhar Rao.

FLOUR POWER: A STEAL AT 10P OFF

Seen in Bangalore, by Anup Bhan.

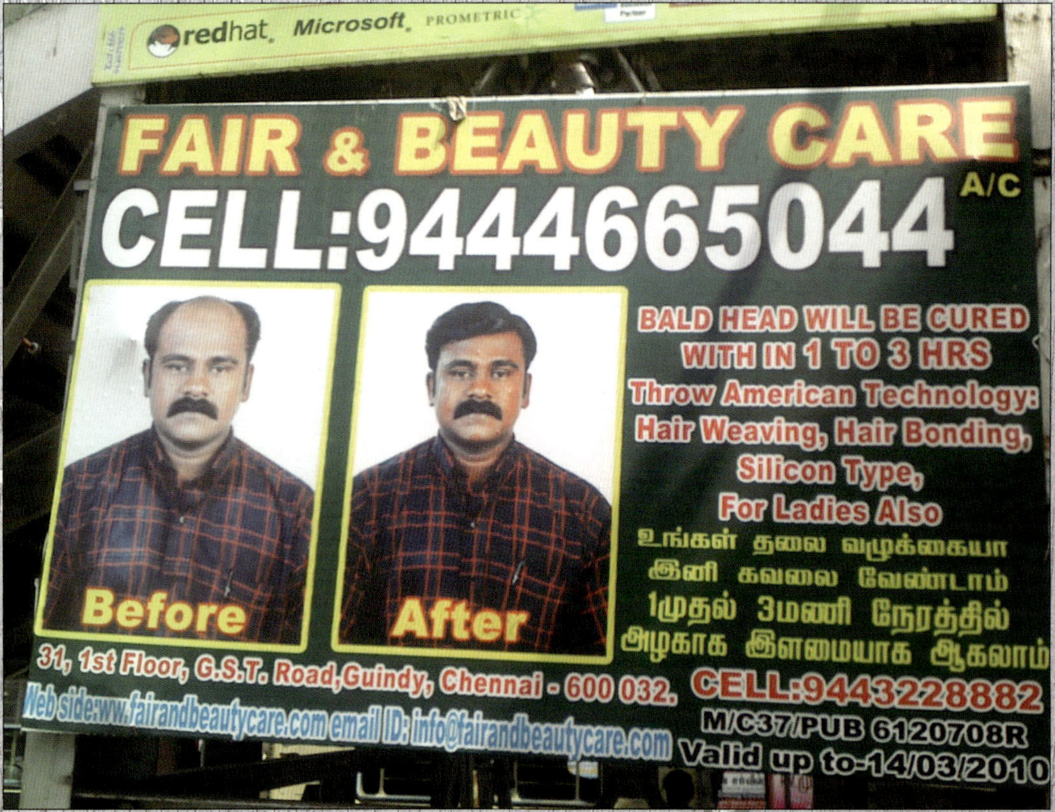

HAIR TODAY, GAIN TOMORROW

Seen in Chennai, by Ashok Rajani.

VISIT FOR A HOLY MEAL

Seen near the Patal Bhuvaneshwar temple in the Pithoragarh district, Uttarakhand by Akshay Kumar Singh.

THEY'RE LOVIN' IT

Seen in Lucknow, by Gagan Kohli.

THE HEIGHT OF HOSPITALITY!

The last Indian dhaba on the border with China is Chitkul, (Himachal Pradesh) which has a population of just 610. Seen by Dr. Nikhils Ghokle.

ONE MAN'S PUBLIC DISPLAY OF AFFECTION IS ANOTHER MAN'S PORN

Seen in a park in Bhubaneswar, by Shubham Jaiswal.

JUST SHUT UP AND DRIVE

Seen in Jamshedpur, Jharkhand, by Amit Bhattacharjee.

CROSS THE ROAD FOR THE CHICKEN

Seen near Kaka Restaurant, in NH-5 Faridabad, Haryana, by Ria.

THE KEY TO SAFETY

Seen ouside a Mall in Bhubaneswar, by Ajay Bisoi.

FOOD YOU WILL LOVE TO BITE INTO

This strange dhaba was seen in Har ki Pauri car parking, Haridwar, by Ashish Sehgal.

PAY PER USE

This interesting poster was seen outside a local 'wine & beer' shop in Gurgaon, Haryana by Nidhi Das.

CLEAR DIRECTIONS

Seen on the highway from Chandigarh to Amritsar, by D.Raveendran.

MULTI-FAITH WARNING

Seen on the roads of Hyderabad, by Mohit Gupta.

WHAT YOU SEE IS WHAT YOU GET

Seen in a Pune restaurant, by Zehnaz L.

A ROSE BY ANY OTHER NAME

Seen outside a temple in New Delhi, by Anu Malhotra.

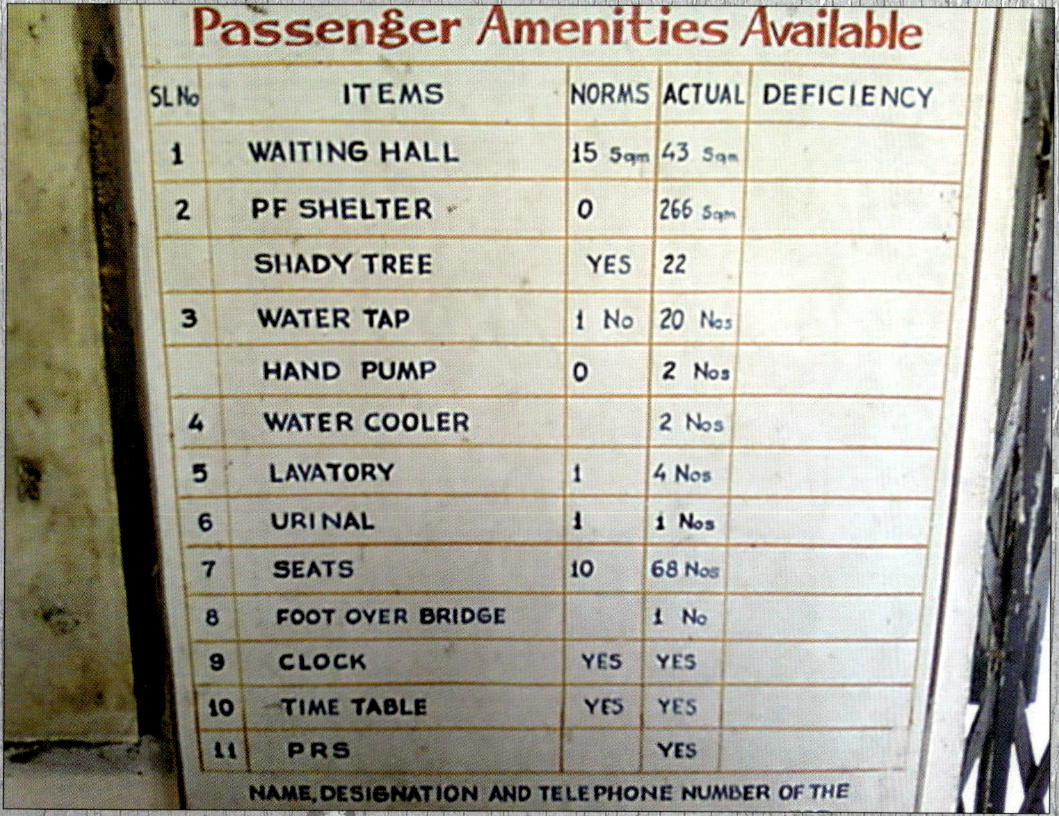

INFORMATION OVERLOADED

Seen at Angul Railway Station in Orissa, by Sukhdev Singh.